GW01417816

The WELFARE STATE

PUTTING THE RECORD STRAIGHT

BY CAREY OPPENHEIM

CPAG LTD, 1-5 BATH STREET, LONDON EC1V 9PY

CPAG promotes action for the relief, directly or indirectly, of poverty among children and families with children. We work to ensure that those on low incomes get their full entitlements to welfare benefits. In our campaigning and information work we seek to improve benefits and policies for low-income families, in order to eradicate the injustice of poverty. If you are not already supporting us, please consider making a donation, or ask for membership details of our membership schemes and publications.

Published by Child Poverty Action Group Ltd, 1 - 5 Bath Street, London EC1V 9PY

© CPAG Ltd, 1994

ISBN 0 946744 67 X

Poverty Publication 87

This book is sold subject to the condition that it shall not, by way of trade or otherwise, be lent, resold, hired out or otherwise circulated without the publisher's prior consent in any form of binding or cover other than that in which it is published and without a similar condition including this condition being imposed on the subsequent purchaser.

The Welfare State: Putting the Record Straight is a revised version of a CPAG briefing entitled Crisis–What Crisis?, published in October 1993.

A CIP record for this book is available from the British Library

Cover design and typesetting: The Bears Communications, 071 272 8760
Design: Devious Designs, 0742 755634
Printing: Crowes, 0603 403349

CONTENTS

ACKNOWLEDGEMENTS   iv

FOREWORD   v

1 INTRODUCTION   1

2 THE SCOPE AND NATURE OF THE REVIEWS   2

3 THE CONTEXT   3

4 SOCIAL SECURITY SPENDING   6
  Patterns of spending   6
  Government forecasts   6
  Why has spending increased?   9

5 THE INTERNATIONAL DIMENSION   12
  The poor relation of Europe   13

6 THE GOVERNMENT'S APPROACH   16
  Better targeting   17
  Means-testing   17
  Tighter restrictions   22
  Age cut-offs   22
  More 'self-provision'   23
  Taxing benefits   27
  'Targeting' lone parents   28

7 CONCLUSION   33

APPENDIX ONE   36

APPENDIX TWO   37

ACKNOWLEDGEMENTS

Carey Oppenheim is research and information officer for the Child Poverty Action Group. She would like to thank Martin Barnes, Fran Bennett, Linda Bransbury, Sue Brighouse, Jean Ellis, John Hills, Emma Knights, Beth Lakhani, John Lyons, David Piachaud, David Thomas and Sally Witcher for their very helpful comments on the first draft. She would like to thank Steve Webb for permission to reproduce Figure 1. She would also like to thank Debbie Sandiford for typing the first draft, Mary Shirley and Jill Bowman for all their work on the manuscript and Renée Harris for editing and producing it.

Foreword

CRISIS – WHAT CRISIS?

The publication of *The Growth of Social Security* came at a time when the gap between rich and poor was at its widest since the Second World War. Nearly a third of all children in the United Kingdom now live in poverty, as does almost a quarter of the population as a whole.[1] Such a situation can be legitimately described as a crisis. But is it the same crisis as that portrayed in *The Growth of Social Security*?

No one, least of all CPAG, would argue that the current social security system is perfect. Like Peter Lilley in his introduction to *The Growth of Social Security*, we want to see a 'constructive national debate … based on the facts'.[2] We do not, however, accept that underlying growth in social security will exceed future growth in the economy. Even on the basis of the figures presented, there is little to support such a view. But there are also grounds for challenging the unduly pessimistic assumptions behind those figures. With a few minor, yet justifiable, amendments to 'the facts' a different picture emerges, with social security expenditure actually falling as a percentage of the Gross Domestic Product (GDP).

The Government's review starts from the premise that social security expenditure is a fixed pot of money which needs to be reduced and then apportioned more accurately in relation to need. As we argue here, expenditure on benefits is largely a reflection of problems or policies elsewhere, like high unemployment, lack of affordable high quality childcare and deregulation of the housing market.

No mention is made in the Government's review of the 'hidden welfare' of tax reliefs and allowances which largely assist the better off. By their exclusion, we are inevitably left with an exercise in the redistribution rather than the reduction of poverty and its close relative, inequality.

The closed nature of the Government's review threatens still further the shared objective of a constructive debate based on the facts. *The Growth of Social Security* is an oasis of rational thought compared with the stormy and murky rhetoric of the months before and after its publication. We have seen the 'deserving versus undeserving poor' debate carried to new extremes, with the Treasury spotlight turned on one group of claimants after another. But sensational stories in the press are a natural counterpart to secrecy. Much could be done to avoid both.

A number of myths urgently need to be challenged. Contrary to popular belief, we do not have a high rate of taxation compared with other industrialised countries, neither do we spend as much as many on social needs. Benefit levels are far from generous, bearing no obvious relation to expenditure requirements. Universal and contributory benefits are already well targeted – even in the narrowest sense of targeting according to income. Ninety-two per cent of expenditure on child benefit, for example, goes to people on middle or low incomes.

Although discussions may focus on who deserves to get benefit and how much, they mask a much more fundamental question about the *role* of social security. At its most extreme, the question being posed is why we need a state-run social security system at all. There are very good answers – but they are based on a much broader role for social security than that currently being suggested by government.

To target (arguably) limited resources on those most in need only makes sense if you accept that social security cannot prevent people falling into poverty, nor help people get out of it. Self-provision makes sense only for those already fortunate enough to be able to provide for themselves via insurance companies who are unlikely to be in a position to take on 'poor risks'. How long before the remaining 'welfare for the poor' becomes poor welfare? The solid societal infrastructure provided by a social security system to which we all contribute and from which we all gain would rapidly disappear.

CPAG believes that social security has a major role to play in preventing poverty and assisting people out of poverty, as well as alleviating poverty once it has struck. Where initial distribution of income is so unequal, social security has an important redistributive role – not only from richer to poorer, but also over the lifecycle and from families without children towards those with children. All these roles are vital. None of them is performed adequately by the current social security system.

Since Beveridge, social security provision has largely evolved in a piecemeal fashion, without any long-term guiding sense of strategy or objective. Benefits are inadequate, even for the minimalist role of alleviating poverty. An increasing emphasis on means-testing creates poverty traps and work disincentives. The role of 'universal' benefits, such as child benefit, in bridging the gap back into work is routinely overlooked. The social security system overall is highly complex, resulting in the failure of many to receive their just entitlement.

Cut after cut has already been inflicted on our social security system. Meanwhile, the tax base has also been cut, leading to a reduction in tax revenue and a transfer of resources from poorer to richer: since 1979 the bottom 10 per cent has seen its income after housing costs drop by 14 per cent, whereas the top 10 per cent has experienced rises of 62 per cent.[3] This trend has to stop.

Of course, social security expenditure has also increased – but primarily because of demands originating outside the social security system itself, rather than to benefit improvements or generosity.

Reducing reliance on social security must not be achieved by making the social security system unreliable. There is no case for cuts and every case for improving support. This is the only way that the crisis in poverty can properly be addressed.

Sally Witcher
Director
Child Poverty Action Group

NOTES

1 Department of Social Security, *Households Below Average Income, A Statistical Analysis 1979-1990/91*, HMSO, 1993.
2 Department of Social Security, *The Growth of Social Security*, HMSO, 1993.
3 House of Commons, *Hansard*, 18 October 1993 cols. 166-7.

Introduction

Over the last year the notion of a deepening 'crisis' in social security spending has been actively promoted by the Government and is widely accepted. But to talk of a 'crisis' is alarmist and has fostered the myth of 'unsustainable spending'. This myth has been used to prepare the ground for cuts in benefits which hit the poorer sections of society, those who have also gained least over the last decade and a half. In our response to *The Growth of Social Security* CPAG shows that social security spending does *not* outstrip the growth in the economy in future years.[1] The recent rise in social security spending is largely a reflection of the length and depth of the recession and changes which lie *outside* the social security system. To focus on the social security budget over all others is to attack the one programme which is more closely geared to the bottom half of the population than any other major public programme. When translated into reductions in social security, the levels of poverty and inequality which have grown so substantially over the 1980s will increase yet again.

There are, of course, important reasons for reforming social security to meet needs more effectively, but such a reform should not be driven by the sole criterion of reducing expenditure. We believe that the public sector borrowing requirement (PSBR) must be tackled through an effective employment strategy, growth in the economy and progressive taxation measures, not by reducing spending on social security.

NOTES

1 Department of Social Security, *The Growth of Social Security*, HMSO, 1993.

2 The scope and nature of the reviews

The Reviews of Public Spending, announced on 8 February 1993 by the Chief Secretary to the Treasury, Michael Portillo MP, are charged with examining the spending of each department, beginning with Education, Health, the Home Office and Social Security, although it is the latter which has been in the spotlight in recent months.[1] The task is intended to be both long-term and short-term. The results are likely to shape the next Conservative manifesto; they will also influence how the Chancellor balances the need to raise taxes against making public expenditure cuts in forthcoming Budgets.

While CPAG welcomes both the Secretary of State for Social Security's Mais Lecture, in which he outlined the future of social security,[2] and the publication of *The Growth of Social Security*,[3] these fall far short of open consultation. By contrast, the 1985 Reviews of Social Security *did* consult openly and received both oral and written evidence. This time, discussions have taken place largely in private, behind closed government doors, with speculation fuelled by a series of highly publicised and arbitrary leaks. Such an approach inevitably causes a great deal of anxiety among claimants who have no way of verifying the truth of particular disclosures. The debate on these issues is of central public concern. We believe that these reviews should be subject to broad and open consultation.

NOTES

1 House of Commons, *Hansard*, 8 February 1993, cols. 681 – 2.
2 Rt Hon Peter Lilley MP, Secretary of State for Social Security, Mais Lecture, 23 June 1993.
3 Department of Social Security, *The Growth of Social Security*, HMSO, 1993.

3 The context

The reviews of the welfare state have been driven by fears of the size of the PSBR. The exact scale and nature of the PSBR has itself been the subject of much debate. Recent reports have suggested that the PSBR might not be quite as high as the £50bn figure anticipated for this financial year. The National Institute for Economic and Social Research argues that borrowing is not excessive in the context of the recent recession and estimates that the PSBR will be £46bn in 1993/4 and £36bn in 1994/5.[1]

A large proportion of the debt can be attributed to the rapid rise in unemployment – not just the cost of benefits for the unemployed, but also the loss of tax and national insurance revenue. The Prime Minister himself has argued that 70 per cent of the PSBR is 'cyclical', ie, attributable to the recession.[2]

The need to borrow has been compounded by lost revenue from a very unequal narrowing of the tax base. Income tax rates have been reduced from 83 per cent to 40 per cent for top-rate taxpayers and from 33 per cent to 25 per cent for basic rate taxpayers over the last decade and a half. Reductions in inheritance tax, capital gains tax, corporation tax, the introduction of independent taxation and tax breaks for savers have also served to narrow the tax base.[3]

Compounding these two main factors have also been some expensive policy mistakes, such as the poll tax, which required vast sums of public money to implement, soften its impact and then to finance its replacement.

While the problem of public finances must be taken seriously, it is essential that any proposals for reforming the social security system be discussed against a background of profound changes in our society. Most importantly, poverty and inequality have increased sharply. The latest government figures show that close to a quarter of the population – around 13.5 million people – are living in poverty (defined by CPAG as below half the average income after housing costs) and that nearly four million of these people are children.[4] Between 1979 and 1990/91, the real income of the poorest 10 per cent (including the self-employed) *fell* by 14 per cent after housing costs, while the average saw their real incomes *rise* by 36 per cent and the richest 10 per cent enjoyed a staggering *rise* of 62 per cent (see Table 1).[5] The broad pattern is clear – the real incomes of the poorest have fallen far behind those of the average over the decade, while the more affluent have experienced remarkable rises in their real incomes.

Table 1: **Percentage changes in real income by decile group 1979 – 1990/91**		
Decile Group Medians	Income before housing costs	Income after housing costs
Decile 1	-1	-14
Decile 2	6	0
Decile 3	11	7
Decile 4	17	16
Decile 5	23	22
Decile 6	27	28
Decile 7	31	33
Decile 8	36	38
Decile 9	43	45
Decile 10	58	62
Note: All estimates are subject to sampling error.		
Source: House of Commons, *Hansard*, 18 October 1993, cols. 166-7.		

This dramatic sharpening of divisions has been caused by increasing inequality in original income (before taxes and benefits have been paid), a result largely of unemployment and the widening dispersion of earnings.

But the tax and social security systems have also become less redistributive since 1985 – ie, less able to narrow the widening gap in original income (see Appendix 1).[6] It is particularly changes in the tax system which account for the weakening of redistribution.

A parliamentary answer shows just how unevenly the cuts in income tax have fallen: if the 1978/79 income tax regime were in place today, a further £31.4bn would be raised (though this takes no account of changes in behaviour). Receiving 48 per cent of the total tax cuts, the top 10 per cent of taxpayers has enjoyed a reduction in its income tax of £6,000 a year, compared to the bottom 50 per cent which has received just 15 per cent of the total tax cuts – an average of £400 a year.[7]

These changes have been accompanied by other new patterns: changing family structures (in particular the growth in the number of lone parents) and an ageing population. The labour market has been substantially reshaped by economic changes: unemployment remains the key economic problem; the security of life-time employment is largely a thing of the past; there has been an increase in temporary and insecure forms of employment; a much higher proportion of women are in paid work and part-time work; and self-employment has increased substantially.

Any review of social security must take on board the increasing depth of impoverishment and social divisions and the social and economic changes of recent years.

NOTES

1 W Hutton, 'The Budget Bamboozlers', The Guardian, 23 August 1993 and N Pain, G Young and P Westway, National Institute of Economic and Social Research, August 1993.
2 House of Commons, Hansard, 5 July 1993, col. 4.
3 Financial Times, 13 July 1993.
4 Department of Social Security, Households Below Average Income, A Statistical Analysis 1979 – 1990/91, HMSO, 1993.
5 House of Commons, Hansard, 18 October 1993, cols. 166-7.
6 Economic Trends, January edition, HMSO, 1994.
7 House of Commons, Hansard, 19 June 1992, cols. 688-9.

4 Social security spending

PATTERNS OF SPENDING

The spotlight has been turned on the welfare state. Since 1979, spending on the welfare state as a whole has grown in real terms. It remained a relatively constant proportion of the GDP over the last decade and a half – at between 23 per cent and 24.7 per cent of GDP until the late 1980s.[1] The latest recession has pushed up the share to 26.4 per cent in 1992/93.[2] However, as Julian Le Grand points out in his analysis of welfare state spending, 'The State of Welfare', when looked at over a longer period (since the Second World War), the rate of growth of welfare state spending as a proportion of national output has slowed significantly since the mid-1970s:

> The increase in the importance of the welfare state relative to other areas of the economy stopped in the mid-seventies.[3]

Within that framework, however, social security has accounted for a growing share of welfare state spending over the last decade and a half. The budget stands at some £80bn for 1993/94, a growth of two-thirds in real terms since 1979.[4]

GOVERNMENT FORECASTS

The Government's paper, *The Growth of Social Security*, examines the growth in spending and sets out some forecasts for future spending in 1999/2000.[5] The Secretary of State for Social Security, Peter Lilley MP, is forthright in his analysis of the implications of the rise in spending:

the underlying growth in social security has exceeded and will continue to exceed growth in the economy;

the underlying growth is above the growth that can be afforded for public expenditure as a whole.

It is these conclusions which provide the background to the Secretary of State's view, clearly stated in his Mais Lecture:

There is no escaping the need for structural reform of the social security system to contain spending.[6]

CPAG challenges both the analyses and the forecasting contained in the report. We contend that first, the Government's own figures do not support its conclusions; secondly, that some of the assumptions in *The Growth of Social Security* are questionable and thirdly, that spending in future years may not be as high as has been suggested.

The Government argues that social security spending has veered out of control. *The Growth of Social Security* figures themselves show that as a percentage of the GDP, benefit expenditure was 9.5 per cent in 1980/81, rising sharply to 11.5 per cent in the mid-1980s (when there was very high unemployment), then falling again to 9.5 per cent in 1989/90, when unemployment dropped. The pattern is uneven, reflecting economic fortunes rather than unrelenting rise in the share of social security spending as a proportion of the GDP. In fact, the extremely rapid growth in social security over the last three years is due primarily to the recession and is not indicative of a trend over the last 15 years.

The Growth of Social Security applies three scenarios to future social security spending in 1999/2000:

   (i)   a continuation of unemployment at current levels of around 3 million;

   (ii) a fall in unemployment of 25 per cent;

   (iii) a fall in unemployment of 50 per cent.

On the first of these scenarios, *The Growth of Social Security* predicts that social security spending will rise from 12.3 per cent of GDP in 1992/93 to 13.5 per cent in 1999/2000. According to the second scenario, *The Growth of Social Security* predicts that social security spending will remain a stable proportion of GDP, rising from 12.3 per cent in 1992/93 to just 12.4 per cent in 1999/2000, and it actually falls to 11.3 per cent in the third scenario, which asumes a fall of 50 per cent in unemployment.

Given the current fall in unemployment, *The Growth of Social Security*'s figures do not support the claim that social security spending will exceed growth in GDP in the future.

Turning to the assumptions, our main cause of concern is the way in which housing benefit expenditure is treated. *The Growth of Social Security* uses *gross* rather than *net* housing benefit expenditure, ignoring its impact on other departmental expenditure. This is not a fair representation of what is happening to public expenditure as a whole. The DSS document itself states:

> Overall growth in expenditure on gross rent rebates is forecast to be 5.5 per cent per annum... *The net effect on public expenditure will be much less than is implied by the growth in gross rent rebates* because Housing Revenue Account surpluses, mainly arising from the assumed higher rents, will considerably reduce the amount of rebate to be paid from public expenditure. *The net growth in public expenditure is forecast to be about 1.3 per cent per annum.*[7] [Our emphasis.]

The Growth of Social Security treats housing benefit expenditure in a way which is exactly the opposite of that applied to residential care spending – where savings accruing to the DSS as a result of the gradual transfer of residential care to the Department of Health are rightly excluded from the DSS budget.

We believe the same approach should be applied in each case. If net housing benefit is used, the increase in social security spending between 1992/93 and 1999/2000 falls by between £1.6bn and £3bn.[8] If we use net housing benefit expenditure and assume that unemployment falls by a quarter (the second scenario) social security spending will *fall* as a proportion of the GDP by the year 1999/2000.

Above all, there is a disparity between the *certainty* of the conclusions ministers have drawn from the figures in comparison with the *uncertainty* of the forecasts. Correspondence between the

DSS and Professor David Piachaud of the London School of Economics, reproduced below, highlights this issue:

> You justify the need for a fundamental review of social security largely in terms of the rapid past and prospective growth in expenditure. There can be little argument about the facts on past growth, although there can be much debate about the reasons. *On prospective growth, there must clearly be a high degree of uncertainty. Yet I have grave doubts about the 'underlying' 3.3 per cent p.a. growth rate that is projected, forecast or expected. With present policies, this figure is in my judgement, unduly high, indeed downright alarmist.'* [Our emphasis.]
> Letter from Professor David Piachaud to Peter Lilley MP, 31.8.93.

> *The Secretary of State shares your view that there is bound to be uncertainty about the future. Different assumptions will inevitably produce different results.* [Our emphasis.]
> Letter from Jane Rentoul, Private Secretary to Peter Lilley MP, to Professor David Piachaud, 16.9.93.

To conclude, assuming that unemployment goes down – even at the modest rate of falling by a quarter – and that the economy continues to grow at the rate set out in *The Growth of Social Security*, and that assumptions are altered to reflect net housing benefit, social security spending will fall as a proportion of the GDP. CPAG does not believe that the growth in social security spending will outpace the growth in the economy. We cannot therefore see any real justification for the bleak picture drawn by the Secretary of State. We would in any case be concerned should the pressure on public spending become the starting point for restructuring social security, rather than identifying how the system can be reformed to meet modern needs most effectively.

WHY HAS SPENDING INCREASED?

While the crisis might not be the kind of crisis portrayed by the Government, underlying expenditure *has* increased and it is important to look at the reasons why.

> Social security and social policy do not exist in a vacuum. The pressures upon each stem from the society which they seek to serve

and these pressures, as much as financial ones, make a review of social security worthwhile.[9]
Alistair Burt MP

The major source of the growth of expenditure has been the increase in the number of claimants.[10]
Peter Lilley MP

As Alistair Burt MP's comments make clear, social security spending totals reflect changes and policies which lie largely *outside* the benefits system. The social security system is in many senses the 'dustbin' for policy changes or failures in other areas. The escalating cost is therefore primarily due not to a more generous social security system, but to increased *demand* for social security.

The demand is the result of three factors: the increase in the number of claimants (pointed out by Peter Lilley above) — particularly unemployed people, lone parents and sick and disabled people; the increased length of time people spend on average on benefit and increased housing costs (which are partly absorbed by benefits). Peter Lilley points to the trebling of the housing benefit budget since 1979:

A large part of that growth reflects the rise in rents in the local authority, housing association and private sectors. There has been a move away from rent controls and subsidising bricks and mortar to subsidising the tenant.[11]

The extension of VAT to fuel, beginning in 1994/95, will have a similar impact. The compensation built into benefit levels will be an inadequate mechanism to protect some groups from rises in their fuel costs. Nevertheless, it will appear as a real rise in social security spending.

The increased pressure for social security reveals a number of difficulties in a range of government policies. The greater reliance of unemployed people, lone parents and sick and disabled people on social security is largely the result of the inadequacies of employment, training and childcare policies (or an interaction between these areas of policy), rather than the failures of social security itself. Deregulation policies — in particular in the field of housing and residential care — have placed a heavier burden on the social security budget, with the result that for an increasing number of people benefits have become the last line of defence against the rigours of the free market.

Social security spending has to be put in context; it can only be dealt with adequately by looking *outside* the confines of social security itself. To a large extent both the causes of increased expenditure on social security and the solutions to it lie beyond the boundaries of the social security system itself.

NOTES

1 J Le Grand, 'The State of Welfare' in J Hills (ed), *The State of Welfare: The Welfare State in Britain Since 1974*, Clarendon Press, 1990.
2 J Hills with the LSE Welfare State Programme, *The Future of Welfare: A Guide to the Debate*, Joseph Rowntree Foundation, 1993.
3 J Le Grand, loc. cit.
4 Peter Lilley MP, Mais Lecture, 23 June 1993.
5 Department of Social Security, *The Growth of Social Security*, HMSO, 1993.
6 Peter Lilley MP, Mais Lecture, 23 June 1993.
7 DSS, op. cit.
8 Letter from Professor David Piachaud of the LSE to Peter Lilley MP, Secretary of State for Social Security, 31 August 1993.
9 Alistair Burt MP, 'Social Policy Beyond Social Security', speech to the Tory Reform Group, 26 June 1993.
10 Peter Lilley MP, Mais Lecture, 23 June 1993.
11 Ibid.

5 The international dimension

Containing the Cost of Social Security – the International Context, recently published by the DSS, is an attempt to place the UK's social security spending in an international context.[1] In fact, the interpretation of the statistics is one-sided and incomplete. While it is true that many member states within the European Community (EC) are trying to contain social security costs, it is important to emphasise a number of points:

- 'Social protection' includes both health and social security spending. The latter includes private sector spending on social security – eg, occupational pensions. This inflates the UK's social security spending in relation to other EC countries, as the UK provides a large proportion of its earnings-related benefits through the private sector in contrast to much of the EC where the state sector performs this role.
- The cutting of expenditure in many EC countries begins from a much higher base than in the UK.
- In general, the approach of other EC states has *not* been to go heavily down the route of means-testing, as in the UK; in fact, some countries are increasing, or already have increased, revenue for 'social protection' through increased contributions.
- The figures in the DSS report are described with barely any reference to changes in unemployment rates and patterns, which provide an essential background to understanding the pressures on the costs of social security.
- Just as in *The Growth of Social Security*, there is a marked discrepancy between the certainty of the conclusions and the uncertainty of the evidence. Under a heading, 'Some Caveats', this document states:

The information contained in this paper should not be considered definitive or comprehensive. It does not attempt a complete overview of social security systems, but concentrates on measures to contain costs.[2]

THE POOR RELATION OF EUROPE

We, too, believe that it is important to put UK spending on social security in an international context. However, our interpretation of the data is rather different. In fact, the UK still has relatively low expenditure on 'social protection' in relation to its European partners.

Table 2: **Expenditure on social protection 1991**	(a) Per capita	(b) Per cent of GDP
Belgium	4,191.2	26.7
Denmark	4,608.7	29.8
France	4,803	28.7
Germany	4,952	26.6
Greece	1,367.8*	20.7*
Ireland	2,240.2	21.3
Italy	3,991.3	24.4
Luxembourg	5,797.3	27.5
Netherlands	5,101.1	32.4
Portugal	1,616.9	19.4
Spain	2,432.9	21.4
United Kingdom	3,653.5	24.7

* 1989

(a) Per capita expenditure in purchasing power standards.

(b) Expenditure as a percentage of GDP.

Source: Social Protection Expenditure and Receipts 1980-1991 Eurostat; House of Commons, *Hansard*, 16 July 1993, col. 669.

This is not something to be proud of, rather it indicates the lower priority the UK has placed on social security and health spending for its citizens. Table 2 sets out social protection spending in each European Community country in 1991, one year later than the DSS data. The UK ranks sixth in terms of spending as a proportion of GDP – far closer to the Mediterranean countries than to the more industrialised countries of the North.[3] Moreover, the UK would rank even lower if private sector spending on social security were excluded.

In an analysis of international social spending by John Hills in *The Future of Welfare*, a guide to the debate, he shows that social spending as a share of GDP has stabilised since 1981:

> The relative scale of Britain's welfare state is smaller than that of most industrialised countries – seventeenth out of the 21 countries listed in the provisional figures for 1989, down from thirteenth in 1981. In the European Community, only Portugal had a lower share. Even allowing for the rapid increase with recession in the last couple of years (which will also have affected other countries), Britain remains well below the OECD average.[4]

When we look at our tax and social security contributions as a proportion of the Gross National Product (GNP), the UK's contributions are again relatively low in comparison with other industrialised countries.[5] We ranked tenth in the Organisation of Economic Co-operation and Development in 1989 (see Table 3), one place lower than in 1979. CPAG believes that, far from the rest of the EC being out of step with the UK, we are out of step with other EC countries which have similar levels of economic output, both in the area of social policy and in social spending.

Table 3: **Taxes and social security contributions as a percentage of GNP at factor cost by rank**

	1979		1989	
	Percentage	Rank	Percentage	Rank
Including Social Security contributions				
Sweden	54	2	66	1
Denmark	54	3	61	2
Norway	56	1	55	3
Netherlands	50	4	51	4
France	46	8	51	5
Austria	49	6	48	7
Germany	46	7	45	8
Finland	37	10	43	9
United Kingdom	39	9	43	10
Italy	30	15	42	11
Canada	34	11	39	12
Greece	32	12	36	13
Japan	26	16	33	14
USA	30	14	32	15
Switzerland	31	13	32	16

Source: Economic Trends, January edition, HMSO, 1992.

NOTES

1 Department of Social Security, *Containing the Cost of Social Security – The International Context*, HMSO, 1993.
2 Ibid.
3 House of Commons, *Hansard*, 16 July 1993, col. 695.
4 J Hills with the LSE Welfare State Programme, *The Future of Welfare: A Guide to the Debate*, Joseph Rowntree Foundation, 1993.
5 *Economic Trends*, January edition, HMSO, 1992.

6 The Government's approach

The Government has a difficult task in its quest to cut social security costs. It is committed to its manifesto promises on maintaining universal child benefit and retirement pension, which together account for about a third of the social security budget. Searching round for other savings is equally hard; as Will Hutton of The *Guardian* put it, 'modifying an already minimalist system is no crock of gold'.[1]

The Secretary of State for Social Security, Peter Lilley MP, proposes to adopt two approaches which he describes as 'better targeting' and 'more self-provision'.[2] But it is important to note that these are driven not just by economic goals but by ideological ones. For those on the right of the Conservative Party, the objective is 'to roll back the frontiers of the welfare state'.[3] The Chief Secretary to the Treasury, Michael Portillo MP, has described it as the ethical dimension of controlling public spending:

> We have a duty to control the size of the State and to reaffirm that the State serves the individual and not the other way round. If the public sector grows relative to the private sector, that chokes off the amount of national wealth to the people who created it. That cannot be right.[4]

But such a view is not held by all those on the government side. We would have much more sympathy, for example, with the approach expressed by Alan Howarth MP:

> The Conservative Party must not be obsessed with reducing public expenditure as an end in itself. Conservatism must not implode into the ideological black hole of the minimal state. Instead, the party should renew a more expansive and generous tradition which

recognises that our society is interdependent, that it is the duty of the strong to help the weak, and that the state acts indispensably on our behalf in the furtherance of that trust.[5]

BETTER TARGETING

The existing array of benefits, contributory, universal and income-related, are rather more targeted than some comment suggests. In aggregate, about 70 per cent of benefit goes to the 30 per cent of the population with the lowest pre-benefit income.'[6] [Our emphasis.]
Peter Lilley MP

'Better targeting' can take a number of forms. It does not necessarily imply means-testing. In his Mais lecture, Peter Lilley MP described targeting in terms of means-testing, tighter restrictions on eligibility or changing the categories for benefit.[7] In many respects a false distinction is made between targeted and universal benefits. For example, you can argue that child benefit – usually described as a universal benefit – is also targeted on children. As Peter Lilley himself concedes in the quotation above, many universal and contributory benefits are, in fact, also well-targeted on income grounds.

Appendix Two includes a table which shows how the recipients of different types of benefit are distributed across the income range. It reveals that only a very small proportion of people receiving non-means-tested benefits has high incomes. The vast bulk are on middle and low incomes.

MEANS-TESTING

It is worth emphasising that the principle of focusing help on the poorest appears at first glance to be the basis for a credible strategy. The view that the principle of universality is no longer sustainable is one which is expressed, with some notable exceptions, by the majority of the most influential media commentators and leader writers. To argue against directing benefits to the poorest *seems* to be flying in the face of common sense and logic. However, the arguments against this approach are in fact powerful and need to be made.

The case against means-tested benefits has been rehearsed many times. They:

- are complex;
- are difficult and expensive to administer;
- create unemployment and poverty traps because benefits are withdrawn sharply as income rises;
- cannot help the 'near-poor' with incomes just above the qualifying thresholds;
- create a disincentive to save;
- are stigmatising to claim;
- reduce many women's independence as they are based on a couple's income;
- often do not reach their targets – ie, a sizeable minority does not claim its entitlements or is inaccurately assessed and therefore fails to get its full entitlement;
- do not provide a secure income as they have to be reassessed each time circumstances change – this does not encourage claimants to take risks in terms of entering the labour market or changing jobs;
- relieve rather than prevent poverty;
- tend to be low because the affluent do not benefit from them and thus are unwilling to fund higher benefits.

In contrast, benefits which do not rely on a means test:

- are secure in a rapidly changing world;
- are not withdrawn when income or families change;
- prevent poverty;
- provide an incentive to work as they are not withdrawn as earnings rise;
- are simple and cheap to administer;
- provide independent incomes for men and women and therefore have less impact on a partner's work decisions;
- have much higher rates of take-up and therefore are more likely to reach those for whom they are intended;
- are well-targeted on income grounds, going to those on middle and low incomes;
- allow us all to have a stake in society.

Commentators who support the move to a more selective system through greater means-testing start from the mistaken premise that the budget for social security is fixed; a point powerfully made by David Piachaud in a Fabian Society pamphlet:

> The question of whether benefits should be means-tested is often put in the form: is it better to provide low benefits to all or give high benefits to those who need them? ... This is entirely misleading. There is not some fixed fund available for social security which the Government is free to distribute as it thinks fit. People pay national insurance contributions that finance the bulk of social security in the expectation of certain rights to future benefits. If such rights were made subject to means-testing, then willingness to pay contributions would inevitably be affected. The evidence that this is so would be obvious if some of those who preach that universalism is dead looked across the English Channel or Atlantic. Continental systems which are largely contributory, with benefits more closely related to what individuals put in than in Britain, provide in general much higher benefits; *systems which are means-tested,* such as AFDC [Aid for Dependent Children] in the USA *provide far less adequately because the prosperous, deeming them to be programmes exclusively for the poor, are unwilling to fund them.* [Our emphasis.][8]

REDISTRIBUTION OVER THE LIFECYCLE

The proponents of means-testing have a narrow view of the role of social security and the needs which it should meet. In a complex society social security inevitably has multiple functions. Research by the London School of Economics shows that around two-thirds of social security spending shifts resources over the lifecycle, and around one third redistributes them between rich and poor.[9] The former is one important way of preventing poverty. The authors write:

> Social security systems redistribute resources both between different individuals and within the lifetimes of the same individuals ... the British social security system does both, with the latter being rather more important. *It would therefore be wrong to look on it as being about just one, or just the other.* [Our emphasis.][10]

An illustration of lifecycle distribution is shown in Table 4. A stereotypical lifecycle is chosen as an example, in this case a single person becoming part of a couple, having children and then retiring. Table 4 shows how social security benefits function to provide extra income at the more vulnerable points over a lifetime.

Table 4: **Lifecycle distribution of social security benefits in 1991**		
Lifecycle	Original income	Original income + benefits
1 adult (non retired)	11,187	12,404
2 adults (non retired)	22,567	23,804
2 adults and 1 child	21,112	22,467
2 adults and 2 children	21,611	23,276
2 adults and 3 children	20,807	23,276
retired couple	6,982	12,074
single pensioner	2,566	5,954
Average income over the lifecycle	15,262	17,593
Adapted from F Coulter, and N Barr, in J Hills (ed), *The State of Welfare*, Clarendon Press, 1990.		

The least well targeted [benefits] on income are child benefit, widow's benefit and industrial injuries benefit of which 30 per cent, 40 per cent and 55 per cent respectively go to the population with the lowest incomes. *However, these benefits are intended to help people with the costs of rearing children,* the loss of a husband and the loss of faculty through injury. [Our emphasis.][11]
Peter Lilley MP

Child benefit provides an example of the issues raised by the debate about means-testing and universality. It is often the first benefit which is picked out as being poorly targeted on income grounds. This is to view the social security system in too narrow a way; child benefit has functions other than this, as admitted by Peter Lilley in the quotation above. It provides cash directly to the parent with prime responsibility, usually the mother; it redistributes over the lifecycle and from those without children to those with; and it provides a contribution from society to the basic costs of all children.

Table 5: **Distribution of child benefit expenditure[a] among families with children by income bands, (adjusted for family size)[b] 1990-91[c]**

Net income of benefit unit (adjusted for family size)[d]	Percentage of child benefit expenditure among benefit units in receipt of child benefit
Before housing costs	*Per cent*
Less than £50	3
£50-£100	16
£100-£200	45
£200-£300	23
£300-£400	8
£400-£500	3
£500 or more	3
After housing costs	
Less than £50	6
£50-£100	27
£100-£200	42
£200-£300	17
£300-£400	4
£400-£500	2
£500 or more	2

Source: Family Expenditure Survey; House of Commons, *Hansard*, 20 July 1993, col. 203.

a. Includes one parent benefit which cannot readily be separated from child benefit in the Family Expenditure Survey data.

b. Income has been adjusted within benefit units using the McClements scales.

c. This represents the latest information available and combines the data for the years 1990 and 1991.

d. Income is in £s per week expressed in January 1991 prices.

However, even taking a narrow view of social security, child benefit is in fact rather better targeted than the figure of 30 per cent quoted by Peter Lilley. It is focused on middle and lower incomes. According to a parliamentary answer (see Table 5), once income is adjusted for family size, 92 per cent of child benefit expenditure goes to families on incomes of less than £300 a week after housing costs, ie, to middle and low income families.

Seventy-five per cent goes to families on incomes of less than £200 a week after housing costs.[12] The reason for this is that families with children tend to cluster in the middle and lower ends of the income distribution.

In health and education the principle of a universal service — funded by all through taxation and providing equal access for all — is widely accepted (although in practice, current policies may well be undermining it). Social security is about cash rather than benefits in kind; nevertheless there is a strong parallel with health and education. We all have a stake in a decently funded and efficiently delivered social security system — we all contribute and we all gain.

TIGHTER RESTRICTIONS

A number of proposals for restricting entitlement to benefits through even tougher tests of eligibility have been floated – such as stricter medical tests for invalidity benefit and tightening the requirement to be available for work. Such measures will inevitably push the system even further down the road of being ungenerous, harsh and discretionary. Witness the rules for young people aged 16 and 17, who no longer have a right to income support but have to leap through several hurdles to be considered for severe hardship payments. This approach, requiring proof of poverty and difficult circumstances, is inevitably bureaucratic and costly.

The social fund is another prime example; the complex administration of loans and discretionary judgements have made this the most expensive benefit to administer. In 1991/92 social fund administration costs amounted to 45.2 per cent of benefit expenditure.[13] Measures along these lines will only further stigmatise the system and decrease the level of take–up.

AGE CUT-OFFS

David Willetts MP has been the prime mover behind the proposal to restrict universal benefits without going down the road of means-testing. His suggestion is to push these benefits to the extremes of the lifespan – child benefit for the under-fives and retirement pension for the over-67s.[14] But in the case of child benefit, while it is right to identify times when women are less likely to be in paid work as particularly difficult, the direct costs of children *increase* as they get older. As Joe Rogaly put it in the *Financial Times*:

> Yet as Mr Willetts will discover as his own toddlers grow up, children get more, not less, expensive to run. Can reduction of benefits for older children really be justified? ...[15]

David Willetts, however, has focused on the *indirect* rather than the *direct* costs of children to parents. To illustrate: Heather Joshi has estimated that the amount of earnings a woman on average earnings foregoes over her lifetime as a result of having two children – the figure is staggering – at over £200,000.[16] Clearly child benefit cannot begin to address these costs and any attempt to do so would confuse its function, which is to make a contribution to the *direct* costs of children. It would be far better to address the opportunity costs for women with young children through childcare, employment and wage measures than through the benefits system.

MORE 'SELF-PROVISION'

The second plank of the Government's approach – increased self-provision – is founded on the belief in a more limited role for government and the view, accepted by some commentators, that the principle of social insurance is no longer valid.

The latter view is based on two factors. First, commentators argue that Beveridge's view of a direct correlation between certain risks such as unemployment, old age, invalidity or sickness and need is no longer true.[17] However, in nearly all cases the primary risks which Beveridge identified – unemployment, disability, and sickness (to which must be added lone parenthood and low pay) – are still closely associated with need. Even old age, where there has been a widening of inequalities in living standards between pensioners, still carries a high risk of low income. Just 9 per cent to 10 per cent of people in receipt of retirement pensions have incomes (adjusted for family size) of £300 a week or more.[18]

An analysis of national insurance benefits and targeting carried out by Stephen Webb of the Institute for Fiscal Studies (see Figure 1) shows that:

> ... between 1980 and 1990 the incidence of national insurance benefit receipt has moved from being concentrated amongst the poorest decile, to being heavily concentrated among the second poorest tenth of the population.[19]

However, while this trend is clearly discernible, the table in fact shows that national insurance benefits remain very much targeted on the poorer groups. This is borne out by a parliamentary answer shown in Table 6. It reveals that contributory benefits are targeted on the middle and lower sections of the income distribution.[20] Only 9 per cent to 10 per cent of individuals receiving contributory benefits have incomes of over £300 a week, once income is adjusted for family size.

Figure 1: **Contribution of national insurance benefits to household income 1970-1990**

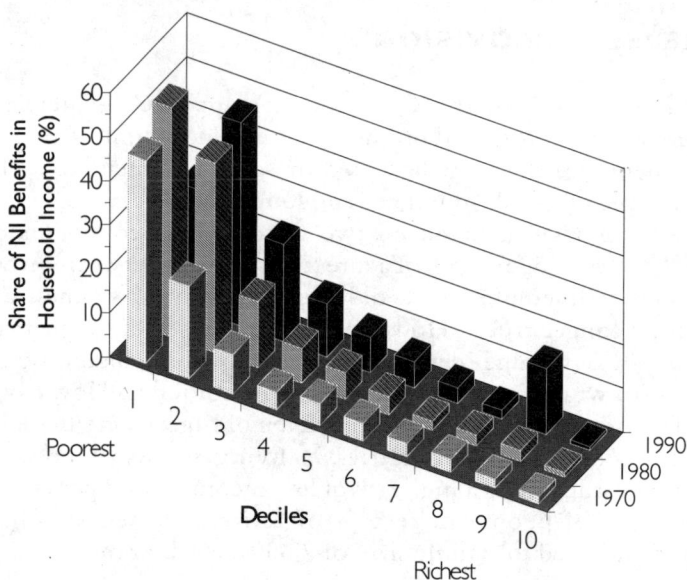

Source: S Webb, 'Social Insurance and Poverty Alleviation: An Empirical Analysis', May 1992, in paper to Beveridge Conference, York University, 1992.

Table 6: **Individuals in benefit units in receipt of contributory benefits distributed across net household income bands (adjusted for family size) 1990/91**

Net income of household (adjusted for family size).	Number of individuals in benefit units where at least one of the contributory benefits is being received.	Percentage of individuals in benefit units where at least one of the contributory benefits is being received.
	000s	Per cent
Before housing costs		
Less than £50	120	1
£50-£100	2530	17
£100-£200	7760	53
£200-£300	2730	19
£300-£400	940	6
£400-£500	330	2
£500 or more	340	2
Total	**14750**	**100**
After housing costs		
Less than £50	410	3
£50-£100	4760	32
£100-£200	5980	41
£200-£300	2230	15
£300-£400	750	5
£400-£500	290	2
£500 or more	330	2
Total	**14750**	**100**

Source: Family Expenditure Survey (FES) 1990/91 in House of Commons, *Hansard*, 23 July 1993, col. 468-9.

Notes

1. Contributory benefits identifiable in the FES are: retirement pension, widow's benefit, unemployment benefit, sickness benefit, statutory sick pay, invalidity benefit, maternity allowance, statutory maternity pay and Christmas bonus.

2. Data are in January 1991 prices.

Secondly, commentators have argued that the national insurance scheme is not really about insurance at all and should therefore be abandoned.[21] While this is certainly true and always has been in an actuarial sense, the evidence shows that the principle has an important resonance in the public mind. People understand the principle of social insurance and feel it gives them a right to claim. It thus represents a fundamental principle of our social security system, that of social solidarity – that all contribute and all gain. Opinion poll research conducted at the time of the 1985 Social Security Reviews showed that 52 per cent of people interviewed thought that national insurance contributions were different from a tax, whereas only 35 per cent thought that they were like a tax. After being told that nine-tenths of national insurance contributions went on social security, 59 per cent of employees and the self-employed thought that their contributions were fair or very fair and only 25 per cent thought that they were unfair.[22]

To move yet further away from contributory benefits – as the Government has done in its latest Budget by reducing the duration of unemployment benefit from a year to six months and restricting invalidity benefit, for example – is to erode an enduring, popular principle: that of contributing in return for a benefit. One reason why the national insurance principle may be popular is that it is earmarked; DEMOS, the new think tank, has suggested that taxation has lost its legitimacy because it is no longer 'democratic'.[23]

The Secretary of State for Social Security has argued that as people become more affluent, they should be able to provide for themselves and opt out of some national insurance benefits.[24] Rumours have suggested that unemployment benefit and the basic retirement pension are possible candidates for such reform. People would still be required to make some contribution to the state scheme, but they would not benefit from the provision.

There are a number of specific difficulties with private schemes:

- the administrative costs are substantial;
- private schemes are less likely to take on poor risks (ie, those people most likely to be in need, such as people with disabilities);
- sharp rises in claims, for example, in a time of recession, would create major difficulties for a private company as it would not

have access to borrowing in the way that the state has;[25]
- the short-term costs to the Exchequer would be considerable as people's contributions declined;
- the middle classes may be less willing to finance state schemes from which they have little or nothing to gain. It follows that state schemes will become harder to finance and thus even less generous – a residual welfare state.

In his work on the welfare state, Le Grand found that middle class interests were very important in preserving the quality of welfare services:

> Services extensively used by the middle classes ... fared substantially better relative to need than those used primarily by the less well-off.[26]

TAXING BENEFITS

Press rumours and leaks over the last year suggested two immediate proposals for taxation: child benefit and invalidity benefit (although the former has been publicly rejected by government ministers). The November 1993 Budget finally brought the speculation about invalidity benefit to an end. It is to be both restricted and taxed.

Both changes have been proposed as short-term measures to save money. In general, CPAG's view is that benefits which replace earnings, such as unemployment benefit, should be treated as part of taxable income. While there may be arguments for taxing invalidity benefit, such a move is hard to justify when the benefit is still so low. However, benefits for meeting costs such as those of children should *not* be taxable. CPAG further sees any proposal to tax child benefit in the life of this Parliament as a breach of the manifesto promise:

> Child benefit will remain the cornerstone of our policy for all families with children. Its value will increase each year in line with prices. Child benefit will continue to be paid to all families, normally to the mother, and in respect of all children.[27]

The arguments against taxing child benefit are strong. Child benefit replaced child tax allowances as well as family allowances –

to tax it would be in effect to tax a tax allowance. To tax child benefit as part of a man's income would sit oddly with recent moves towards independent taxation. Child benefit would therefore be taxed as part of the woman's income – either at all rates of income tax or just at the higher rate of 40 per cent. To tax child benefit at all rates of income would mean a substantial cut in its value to middle and lower income families. Taxing child benefit would also create a disincentive for women to work, as women's labour market behaviour is particularly sensitive to disincentive effects;[28] it would be perceived as taxing families with children more heavily than others; and child benefit would lose its administrative efficiency. If it were to be taxed as part of the woman's earnings it would raise little money – around £600m in total and just £30m if it were taxed only at the higher rate.[29] This is because a large number of women fall below the tax threshold and few have earnings high enough to attract the top rate of tax. CPAG believes that any increase in revenue should be met by all taxpayers, rather than just families with children.

'TARGETING' LONE PARENTS

Recent, ferocious, debate about lone parenthood has been given a new fillip by the fall-out from the Government's 'Back to Basics' campaign. Lone parents have rarely been out of the headlines over the last few months, with suggestions from ministers and MPs ranging from that of the Home Secretary, Michael Howard – to cap the welfare benefits of lone parents with more than one child – to offering only temporary hostel accommodation to lone parents (the latter approach implicit in the homeless review announced by Sir George Young on 20 January 1994). Single mothers, especially teenage mothers, have been facing the harshest glare of the spotlight. In fact, although they make up the fastest growing group among lone parents, single mothers are a minority of all lone parents.

Table 7 shows how lone parents are divided between different groups; the majority are lone parents because of divorce or separation.

There has also been a growing view among some politicians and sections of the media that it is the benefit and housing system which encourages people to become or remain lone parents. A very small proportion of mothers *may* get pregnant to achieve the

Table 7: **Estimated numbers of lone parent families in 1971 and 1991**

Type of family with dependent children	Number (thousands)		% of lone parent families	% of all families
	1971	1991*	1991	1991
Lone mothers				
single	90	440	34	6.4
separated	170	250	19	3.6
divorced	120	430	33	6.3
widowed	120	80	6	1.2
Lone mothers	500	1,200	92	17.5
Lone fathers	70	100	8	1.4
Lone parents	570	1,300	100	19.0
Married couple families (includes some cohabiting couples)				81
All families		6,840		100

* Provisional figures (rounded) for 1991.

Source: A Garnham and E Knights, *The Child Support Handbook*, CPAG Ltd, 1993.

status of an adult or to get a home. If this is so it is a reflection of the society in which they live and the lack of opportunities it offers for self-fulfilment.

In fact there is no hard evidence whatsoever to support this claim. A recent report by the Institute of Housing shows that the correlation between having a child and seeking council housing is 'at best tenuous'.[30] The perpetuation of this view betrays a highly simplistic understanding of human motivation and a failure to grasp the realities of living on income support for long periods of time. Dr Bea Cantillon of the Centre of Social Policy at Antwerp University in Belgium argues:

Scientific research has demonstrated that the influence of financial stimuli on human behaviour is probably less than is generally thought ... Decisions regarding the organisation of family life are influenced by a multiplicity of social, cultural, and psychological factors. The financial aspect (including social protection) is only one of them.[31]

The high proportion of lone parents reliant on income support (over 70 per cent) is not a product of the generosity of this benefit, but arises because they are trapped into staying on it. Nine out of 10 lone parents are women. They are trapped on benefit for a number of reasons: the scarcity of affordable childcare provision; the costs of working (eg, travel, lunch, clothing costs); the low wages they command in the labour market; the uncertainty involved in making the shift from income support to work and the unemployment trap which prevents women moving from income support into work – for example, the loss of free school meals and help with mortgage interest for owner-occupiers.

Two concrete measures have so far emerged from the morass of leaks. The first is a positive, though limited, measure – the introduction of an earnings disregard for childcare costs, applying to families in work who are receiving such benefits as family credit, disability working allowance and housing benefit. It can give up to £28 a week for a family with a child under 11, but it is not a voucher. Although it is an important recognition that lack of affordable childcare acts as a crucial barrier preventing women, in particular lone parents, from entering paid work, it will in fact help only 150,000 people.[32]

The second measure is a negative one. Sir George Young has put forward proposals to end the right of homeless people to be statutorily rehoused in permanent council accommodation under the homelessness legislation. Instead, they will have a right to temporary accommodation for a limited period only. This measure will only increase the hardship faced by homeless people and, in particular, lone parents.

Government must primarily deal with society as it is.[33]
Alistair Burt MP

Like Alistair Burt, CPAG believes that we cannot turn the clock back but must accept changes in family patterns and adjust policies accordingly to protect lone parents and their children from poverty. Tackling the high reliance of lone parents on income support must involve looking at ways of supporting lone parents to enter or return to the labour market when they choose to do so, *not* to cut support which is already meagre. Any attempt to reduce benefit entitlement for lone parents will not increase a mother's chances of working when the obstacles are so great. It will simply penalise the parent who is looking after the child rather than the absent parent and, above all, it will inevitably penalise the child, a fact all too frequently overlooked.

NOTES

1 The *Guardian*, 23 April 1993.
2 Rt Hon Peter Lilley MP, Secretary of State for Social Security, Mais Lecture, 23 June 1993.
3 D Willetts, *The Age of Entitlement*, Social Market Foundation, 1993.
4 Speech by Rt Hon Michael Portillo MP, 19 May 1993.
5 The *Observer*, 14 November 1993.
6 Peter Lilley MP, Mais Lecture, 23 June 1993.
7 Ibid.
8 D Piachaud, *What's Wrong with Fabianism?*, Fabian Pamphlet 558, Fabian Society, 1993.
9 J Falkingham et al, *William Beveridge versus Robin Hood: Social Security and Redistribution over the Lifecycle*, STICERD, 1993.
10 Peter Lilley MP, Mais Lecture, 23 June 1993.
11 Ibid.
12 House of Commons, *Hansard*, 20 July 1993, col. 203.
13 Department of Social Security, *Departmental Report: The Government's Expenditure Plans 1993/94 to 1995/96*, HMSO, 1993.
14 The *Guardian*, 23 April 1993.
15 *Financial Times*, 9 February 1993.
16 H Joshi, 'The Cost of Caring', in C Glendinning and J Millar (eds), *Women and Poverty in Britain: The 1990s*, Wheatsheaf, 1992.
17 Bill Robinson, *Financial Times*, 3 August 1993.
18 House of Commons, *Hansard*, 23 July 1993, cols. 468-9.
19 S Webb, 'Social Insurance and Poverty Alleviation: An Empirical Analysis', paper delivered to Social Security 50 Years After Beveridge conference, York University, 1992.
20 H Joshi, op. cit.
21 *Financial Times*, 9 February 1993.
22 Reform of Social Security, Background Papers, Vol. 3, Cmnd. 9519, HMSO, 1985.
23 G Mulgan and R Murray, *Reconnecting Taxation*, DEMOS, 1993.
24 Peter Lilley MP, Mais Lecture, 23 June 1993.
25 *IFS Update*, Spring 1993.
26 J Le Grand, 'The State of Welfare' in J Hills (ed), *The State of Welfare: The Welfare State in Britain Since 1974*, Clarendon Press, 1990.
27 Conservative Party Manifesto, *The Best Future for Britain*, Conservative Central Office, 1992.

28 F Coulter and N Barr 'Social Security, Solution or Problem?', in J Hills (ed), op. cit.

29 House of Commons, *Hansard*, 21 June 1993, col. 13 and 7 July 1993, col. 156.

30 The *Guardian*, 6 October 1993.

31 Dr Bea Cantillon, 'Family, Work and Social Security', unpublished paper delivered to Social Security 50 Years After Beveridge conference, Vol. 5 paper, York University, 1992.

32 House of Commons, *Hansard*, 1 December 1993, col. 1041.

33 Rt Hon Alistair Burt MP, 'Social Policy Beyond Social Security', speech to Tory Reform Group, 26 June 1993.

7 Conclusion

This publication has concentrated on the case against cutting social security expenditure. Contrary to the Government's view, we are not facing a crisis in social security spending. The Government's own figures show that we *can* afford our social security system for years to come if the economy continues to grow and unemployment continues to fall. The case for cuts has not been made. We have explored the arguments against means-testing and increasing self-provision. If the Government chooses to pursue this approach it can only mean further impoverishment and inequality.

We are, however, facing a crisis in relation to the rise in poverty and inequality. And it is *this* crisis which should be the starting point for the reform of social security.

CPAG's policies are not described here in detail. Instead, we outline some key points which we believe should underpin any review of social security.

- The reform of the social security system should not be driven by expenditure control but by an attempt to respond to the economic and social challenges which face us today.
- It is essential to include tax reliefs and allowances alongside social security benefits in any discussion about the extent of state support and who benefits from it. Many tax reliefs and allowances benefit the better off in particular. To exclude them is in effect to impose the costs of meeting the public debt on those who are least able to pay for it and who have profited least from the 1980s' boom.
- An alternative strategy for social security should not look at benefits alone. The demand for social security can only be tackled with an active employment strategy (including

childcare, hours of work, and training); by enhancing the opportunities for people to support themselves in whole or in part (by combining benefits and earnings); and by controlling the rising costs, such as rent, which are met by benefits.

- Our existing social security system is inadequate to address present needs. We believe that rather than cutting the social security budget, more revenue needs to be raised to improve the level of benefits. This should be done by increasing taxation in a progressive manner, eg, by abolishing the national insurance ceiling and raising direct taxes (in particular for the more affluent), and restricting all tax allowances and reliefs. The Government has moved in the right direction in relation to tax reliefs – the November 1993 Budget announced the restriction of tax relief on mortgage interest payments and the married couple's allowance to 15 per cent from April 1995. However, CPAG would support shifting the savings from these two measures to the creation of a benefit for low income home owners and improving the level of universal child benefit.

- Indirect taxation should not be extended. It is a less progressive method of taxing people than direct taxation. If the scope of VAT is widened to other basic necessities such as food and clothing, the poorest will be hit very hard.

- The social security system has a number of roles: to protect poor people; to redistribute from rich to poor, from those without children to those with children; from men to women and over the individual lifecycle. The broad principles for a comprehensive social security system are set out in the box opposite.

Survey after survey of public attitudes have shown that there is widespread support for a well-funded welfare state. It is time that the Government's policies started reflecting this consensus.

- Social solidarity should underpin our benefits system: collective security against risks such as unemployment or sickness.
- Responsibility for caring for children and others should be shared by society as a whole.
- Reducing inequalities between rich and poor.
- Maximising opportunities for self-support by increasing access to the labour market and reducing unemployment and poverty traps.
- Preventing poverty as well as alleviating it.
- Tackling poverty by providing adequate levels of benefits.
- Individual autonomy – non-means-tested benefits should be paid on an individual basis so that women as well as men, carers as well as disabled people, can claim benefits in their own right.
- There should be rights to benefits rather than dependence on discretionary judgements.
- Equal access and treatment regardless of sex, race, marital status, sexual orientation, or disability.
- Simplicity and flexibility.
- Social integration – benefits should not be socially divisive or stigmatising.

Sources: C Oppenheim, Poverty the Facts, CPAG Ltd, 1993;

R Lister, The Exclusive Society, CPAG Ltd, 1990;

N Barr and F and Coulter, 'Social Security, Solution or Problem?', in J Hills (ed), The State of Welfare, Clarendon Press, 1990.

Percentage distribution of total original and post-tax income of households, adjusted for family size, broken down into quintile groups (fifths)

Original income	1979	1985	1992
Quintile Group	%	%	%
Bottom	2.4	2.5	2.1
2nd	10	7	6
3rd	18	17	15
4th	27	27	26
Top	43	47	50
Post-tax Income			
Quintile Group			
Bottom	9.5	8.6	6.5
2nd	13	13	11
3rd	18	17	16
4th	23	23	23
Top	37	39	44

Source: *Economic Trends*, January edition, HMSO, 1994.

Distribution of benefit recipients across quintiles of household income (adjusted for family size) 1990/91

Before housing costs

Quintiles	1	2	3	4	5	Total
	%	%	%	%	%	%
Contributory benefits	30	29	19	13	10	100
Non-contributory benefits	27	24	21	16	11	100
Income-related benefits	56	30	9	4	1	100
Child benefit	23	22	23	18	14	100
Retirement pension	31	31	17	12	9	100
All benefit units	20	20	20	20	20	

After housing costs

Quintiles	1	2	3	4	5	Total
	%	%	%	%	%	%
Contributory benefits	27	27	19	14	12	100
Non-contributory benefits	28	25	21	16	10	100
Income-related benefits	56	29	9	4	2	100
Child benefit	23	24	23	18	12	100
Retirement pension	27	29	17	13	13	100
All benefit units	20	20	20	20	20	

Source: Family Expenditure Survey (FES), 1990/91.

1. Quintiles are successive fifths of the income distribution from bottom to top. Quintile values are: £114, £116, £224 and £312 (BHC)

£91, £139, £193 and £270 (AHC).

2. Data are in January 1991 prices.

POVERTY: THE FACTS

CHILD POVERTY ACTION GROUP

Carey Oppenheim

Poverty: the facts presents the latest statistics on the nature and extent of poverty in the UK. This new and fully updated edition has been much expanded to include fuller coverage of such topics as: debates on the definition of poverty; government and other statistics; causes and consequences of poverty; poverty in relation to race and gender; deprivation in Scotland, Wales, Northern Ireland and in the English regions; international comparisons.

Fully illustrated with graphs, tables, maps and photographs, *Poverty: the facts* is the most comprehensive, authoritative and accessible assessment of poverty in contemporary Britain.

160 pages   1990   0 946744 28 9   £5.95

Please send me _____ copy/ies of *Poverty: the facts* @ £5.95 each (incl p&p) £_____

I enclose a donation of £_____ towards CPAG's work

I enclose a cheque/PO for £_____, payable to CPAG Ltd

Name _____

Address _____

_____

_____

_____ Postcode _____

Please send cash with order to CPAG Ltd, 1-5 Bath Street, London EC1V 9PY

Europe:
for richer or poorer?

Robin Simpson and
Robert Walker (eds)

**CHILD
POVERTY
ACTION
GROUP**

Now that the Maastricht Treaty has been ratified, the time
has come for Europe to face the consequences for social
policy and the poor.

The authors examine not only the Social Chapter, but also
moves to guarantee a minimum income and services for
children throughout the EC. They analyse the different
social policy traditions – including detailed comparisons of
family benefits and childcare provisions – within each
member state, the geography of poverty throughout the
Community, and tendencies towards 'Fortress Europe'.
Uniquely, this analysis extends to the evolution of social
policy in Eastern Europe, and the global impact of EC
commercial policy on poorer countries outside the
Community.

In this challenging collection, the contributors (from the EC
and beyond) consider whether this 'marriage' of member
states will benefit primarily commerce, the workforce, or *all*
residents of the European Community.

144 pages   0 946744 55 6   December 1993   £6.95

- -

Please send .... copy/ies of *Europe: for richer or
poorer?* @ £6.95 each (incl p&p).

I enclose a cheque/PO for £ .... payable to CPAG Ltd

Name ....

Address ....

....

.... Postcode ....

**Return payment with order to CPAG Ltd,
1-5 Bath Street, London EC1V 9PY**